Ours

A poetic exploration of
Homeland/Motherland

Contributors:
Maureen Duffy, Jana Russ, Robert Jaggs-Fowler,
Sue Knight, Andrew Barber, Pierre Le Gué, Walt Pilcher,
Poorvaja Rajagopalan, Jo Reah, Janet Dean,
Nicola Beeston, Farzana Marie, Robert J Miles,
Frances Andrews and Brian Burchill

ISBN: 978-1-909163-26-3
Cover Design by Paula Ann Murphy

License Notes

The right of the contributors to be identified as the authors of the works within this book has been asserted by them in accordance with the Copyright, Designs and Patents Act 1998.

Introduction

A collection of poems from professional and non-professional contributors put together from the winners of our charity homeland/motherland poetry competition.

The collection will donate 10% of its sales to the WWO, the WorldWide Orphans foundation (**wwo.org**).

The WWO is an international charity and as such is perfectly suited to benefit from this, an international poetry collection.

Fantastic Books Publishing is very proud to be involved with such a worthy and dedicated charity.

Dedication

This collection is dedicated to the memory of Brian Berisford Burchill (1932 – 2008), a hugely talented artist, poet and author who sadly passed away before this collection was published. We would like to thank his widow Bea Burchill for allowing us to publish Brian's poems in this collection.

Brian left us this wonderful insight into how he thought about his art, particularly his landscape paintings;

'I am interested in landscape, not in a representational way, but in a form based on my experiences of landscape. I do not paint from nature - rather I re-assemble images in my mind's eye then commit them to painting.'

'What I find most interesting about landscape is a sense of mystery, of time and the 'spirit' of the place. These are difficult to depict with a naturalistic approach. Therefore I feel the need to 'invent' a place in order to capture these feelings.'

Snapshot by Maureen Duffy

Sorting through the old snaps I'd brought you
you remembered perfectly the stout woman
squatting beside the breakwater, stockinged legs
flung out on the sand: 'Mrs Permain!' you said
effortlessly reaching back seventy years to when
I was too young to remember. This was
our childhood, you seven years older, and now
I bring you these blurred records you love, our
past, turning them over, holding them close
for scrutiny: 'Oh yes, that's Nellie next door.'
Yet you can't recall what I said minutes
ago. Does it matter? You are so happy
in our game of remembrance. 'Bring me
some more,' you say,'next time you come.'
And I will. Oh I will, before that light is snuffed
out.

Maureen Duffy (born in 1933 in Worthing, Sussex, UK) is a notable contemporary British poet, playwright and novelist. She has also published a literary biography of **Aphra Behn**, and **The Erotic World of Faery** a book-length study of eroticism in faery fantasy literature.

After a tough childhood, Duffy took her degree in English from King's College London. She went on to be a schoolteacher from 1956 to 1961, and edited three editions of a poetry magazine called the sixties. She then turned to writing full-time as a poet and playwright after being commissioned to produce a screenplay by Granada Television. Her first novel, written at the suggestion of a publisher, That's How It Was (1962), was published to great acclaim. Her first openly lesbian novel was **The Microcosm** (1966), set in the famous lesbian Gateways club in London.

Her latest publication, '**Environmental Studies**' is available now. Show your support and grab yourself a copy!

Apples from Donji Vakuf by Jana Russ

Zenaida, a teacher,
wants to take the books.
I can understand this-
but there are too many books
and the snipers on the road
target slow movers,
women heavy laden.
She takes, instead, all the apples
from a tree in front of where
Kafedzic's house used to be.
She wanted Kafedzic's
Cat, as well-
but it hissed,
and would not come.
On the ride to Rijeka,
in a rusty bus, leaking oil,
she shares the last apple

with Hana, the girl in the blue
scarf, whose father,
a math professor,
was taken from Sarajevo
the month before.
Neither of them smiles, but
they eat that apple
down to the core,
and they eat the core, the seeds,
eat even the stem.
I cannot understand this-
no matter how I try.
In Rijeka they tell us that this
is the way of things. Books, cats,
homes, even apples-come and go,
and come and go again.
We can only try
to understand.

One of our professional contributors, Jana Russ teaches World Literature, World History, Asian History, Humanities, and Writing at the University of Akron.

East Shanghai by Jana Russ

One more concrete Mao blesses these people,
his outstretched hand conducting
martial airs out of the morning.
In the grassless yard, under stunted sycamores,
a tiny lady in white pyjamas is
dancing with her sword.
On the street, bicycles beep and call to each other
a musical, lost in the endless
cacophony of traffic.
In the impersonal shadow of glass skyscrapers
a blind beggar plays his flute
to his wooden bowl.
Two tiny girls, all pink ribbons and pigtails,
swing homeward hand in hand
chanting lessons.
The bamboo grove whispers a secrets to the
old men in the red pagoda who
dream over their tea.

One of our professional contributors, Jana Russ teaches World Literature, World History, Asian History, Humanities, and Writing at the University of Akron. This is her second poem in the collection.

An Ex-Pat's Lament by Robert Jaggs-Fowler

(With apologies to Robert Browning)

Oh to be in England
now that winter's there;
for, whilst you freeze in England,
think of me and have a care.
There, the deciduous trees are leafless,
whilst chill, northern winds blow, I guess;
and robins sit, fluffed up, on snowy boughs
in England – now!
And after Guy Fawkes Night, Christmas follows:
when, with mulled wine and mistletoe, sorrows
are forgotten around crackling log fires;
whilst children give snowmen carrot noses,
and carols are sung in the streets by choirs
stamping cold feet; their ears red as roses.
I miss steamy windows, and candle light,
and the hoar frost that forms in the night.
I yearn to wear coats and scarves made of wool,
or dress in Black Tie for a winter's ball.
Choosing this Mediterranean heat,
against England's seasons is bitter sweet.

Another of our professional contributors, Robert has many literary achievements under his belt. The winner of the Lincoln Book Festival Prize for fiction in 2005 and the Fathom Prize for poetry in 2010, Robert is currently working on his debut novel and second collection of poetry.

Grown-ups? by Sue Knight

Grown-ups had made us
Bomb sites to play on
Wasn't that grand?
They'd sown the sea
With fireworks
To explode on the sand
Us kids played at war
But who were the baddies?
Now no-one was sure
Was it the Germans?
The big boys said No
Baddies were Russians
But how did they know?
Don't call people Enemies!
Dad said it with passion
We didn't go shopping
We went for our rations
Daddy went to work
Six days of seven
To Silverdale,
Jordanthorpe

Planning new Eden
We always found mummy
At home, in the kitchen
Then farewell Coles Corner
Au revoir trams
Goodbye bomb site
Hello building site
The brave new world began.

Grown-ups soon made us
Landmines to play on
Sunk into sand
Finely adjusted for leg
Or small hand
Us kids played at war
But who were the baddies?
Now no-one was sure.

Sue Knight is a writer of short stories and poems. She and her husband Colin live on the south coast where she is an active member of the local Jehovah's Witness congregation. She can be contacted via her blog at **www.sueknight2000.blogspot.com**

Lietuva by AV Barber

Oh nation proud,
With voice set free.
I hear you calling,
To come to thee.
You call my name,
This wandering son.
I hear your cries,
To make you one.
And with your passion,
And through your pain,
You fought for freedom,
To hear your name.
Then from your shores,
I journeyed far,
But in my heart,
You always are.
So now I'm calling,
With heart set free,
Hear my voice,
I call to thee,
Lietuva!

For A.V. Barber, poetry is merely a means of expression. His original style of combining poetic passages with free flowing prose has been developed purely as a means of giving a little of himself to words – and always with some hope of making a difference. Well-travelled with an unquenchable thirst for knowledge, Andrew Barber finds a style all of his own. By utilising his observations on life, he presents a perspective of everyday living to which everyone can relate. Andrew is another of our professional contributors. His latest project, 'Lion Hearts' can be seen here (**www.avbarber.com/lion-hearts**)

Best of British by AV Barber

Long, grey days with brollies dance,
And to think I could have gone to France.
A seaside holiday with promenade and piers,
Cockle shells, candy floss, blood, sweat, and tears.
The space for long walks, and a chance to respire,
Move over luv, I need time by the fire.
Fish and chips, mushy peas, pies, coughs, and flu,
That curry's gone through me – quick, where's the loo?
Okay, I've had it, I'm off to the pub,
There's happy hour, footy, and plenty of grub.
The test match was halted, bad light has stopped play,
The forecasts not good, there's rain on the way.
Anyone for tennis? Croquet is such fun,
Cream teas with strawberries, scones, and a bun.
Black cabs, red buses, Big Ben, and The Tower,
Running for cover 'cause here comes a shower.
Next year, I'm off to the streets of Marseilles,
It's already booked, I've got two weeks in May.

Andrew is another of our professional contributors. This is his second poem in the collection. His latest project, 'Lion Hearts' can be seen here (**www.avbarber.com/lion-hearts**)

October 1962 by Pierre Le Gué

That month I thought we'd never see the spring.
With Castro and Khrushchev and Kennedy,
Cuba was on the map like nowhere else
In those few autumn days - just one weekend
That came and went so fast. The crisis grew.
We watched the news as hour by hour the ships,
The Russian fleet and JFK's blockade,
Seemed set to fight, then stopped - right on the brink
Of war. 'The other guy just blinked' they said,
But now we know that both sides saw the light
In time to make the world a safer place,
If only for a while. Between the crews
Bourbon and vodka passed instead of shells.
But - there'd be other times and other days
When ideologies and motherlands
Or fatherlands and leaders would recede,
And stark destruction move to centre stage
In people's minds. So far it's worked, but still
The danger lurks, and waits to be renewed
The moment memory fades, and wisdom learned
Falls foul of ignorance or arrogance and greed.

Pierre is a retired teacher who has been reading and watching science fiction since 1947. He has had items published in various poetry anthologies, specialist journals and local newspapers.

Hercules in Dutch by Walt Pilcher

Hercule Poirot from Brussels sprouts
And plants himself in London
With Captain Hastings as his scout
And capable Miss Lemon

Detecting crimes and miscreants
Across the English map
Athwart benighted salience
The Chief Inspector Japp

By Scotland Yard he's held in awe
The criminals all rue him
No plot too thick or threat too raw
Can foil him or subdue him

Perceiving all the subtle clues
The paragon of minds
His methods and his prey each use
Grey cells of different kinds

But lo there comes a season black
A case he cannot fathom
Hercule prepares his best attack
Alors, a mental spasm

Torn with doubt, which thread to follow?
Vacillation awful
Friends and foes with laughter hollow
See the Belgian waffle

Walt Pilcher lives in Greensboro, NC (USA), with his wife, Carol, an artist. During his apparel industry career he moonlighted as a fiction writer, later adding poetry and songwriting with pieces appearing in a range of publications. He divides his time between family (six grandchildren), church, writing, golf and learning guitar.

India by Poorvaja Rajagopalan

Everywhere are grass stains growing
pains, of the rice we eat and the cotton
for our dresses.
Everywhere are emerald trees ruby
leaves, ponds of black silver where the
elephants bathe. The mahoots dress in lungis and
wade into black silver
with elephants like iron and men like earth
and elephant eyes, soft human eyes
as they bathe in the black silver
made from emerald trees.
Somewhere there are tigers, live tigers
Burning Tygers, with fire pelts and eyes like
beer, like gold.
They blink, they yawn, on kitty paws
with fire pelts as soft as down
setting the forests aflame
emerald trees ruby leaves licked by
Tyger Tyger gold.
Everywhere are tigers, dead tigers
festering, moldering

the fleas and the children eat off the pelts
the festering, the moldering
and Tyger Tyger eyes are dead
in my hand, they can't see the trees the
leaves, and the fleas and the children are
starving.
Everywhere are dirt roads, brick roads
living roads, heaving with life
spilling vomit on the floor; mop it up with
blue tarpaulin and child's hands
and wade through the
festering, the moldering
for some dead tiger alms. Life
rots like the dead, brown like dust
picking meat off dead tiger skins.
Everywhere is
the smell of rain, like a river in the sky, like
pebbles and pond and great green fish
the perfume of wet animal, wet tree
wet sparkling coconut flags. In the rain
the trash smells trashier, earth smells
earthier, sky smells like sky and
ground like ruby leaves.

Everywhere are chains, steel chains,
chains in flowers so you don't
see that they're chains. Chains on our feet, chains on our
minds, chains on our chairs and our cows and the
way we smile.
Somewhere are the keys
not in a place where dragons roar, a place where
Tygers Burn alive, where the elephants are in
black silver – this place.
This place – where there is bitter, and there is
mango-coconut sweet, and
this place where
Everywhere,
I am home.

Poorvaja Rajagopalan is a high school student doing her first-year IB diploma course. She lived for eight years in the United States, before moving to India with her parents. Her passions are reading, writing and history. Poorvaja is the grand prize winner of the competition that produced this collection. Our celebrity judge Maureen Duffy said of Poorvaja's poem;
'I particularly liked Poorvaja's imaginative use of language and imagery.'

For the love of the country by Jo Reah

For the love of the country
and hate of the town
I felt my mood
drop down and down.
The place of peace
where I was contented,
was blown up by men
and now lies fragmented.
I don't want to live
in pop music street –
my spiritual home
is a grassy retreat.
I'm savagely mourning
the death of the leaf,
my head aches with thunder
resounding my grief.
I'm down on the floor
of the kitchen again,
I can function no longer
in plastic terrain

so I breathe in the blankness
and choke on the pain.
Pain is my master
again and again.
For the love of the country
and hate of the town
my mood dropped down
and down
and down...

Jo Reah has been a poet all her life. Her love of nature and animals is reflected in her poetry, as is her experience of psychiatric illness and social isolation. Most of her life, she has lived in the north of England, though she has spent time in Sussex. She trained as a psychiatric nurse in Sedgewick, then moved to Manchester before settling in Sheffield where she now lives with her rescue dog, Milly.

Land of the Persimmon by Janet Dean

Where the ebony grows
On a wide flat plain
The Micmac tribe is at the
Fish-spearing place
The orange fruit ripen in the sun
The juice spills down on
Algonquin man

How many moons before you came?
We would not know.
The moon rises, falls;
Then the sun.
What was the point of counting?
We understood the land,
It owned us.

Through the trial and error of our ancestors,
We found the sweeter fruit,
And tamed the cattle.
We spoke to one another;
Rhythmic sounds, tales of deed and conflict,
Mysteries of being.

You wrote our names – Mahican, Shawnee, Ojibwas -
Without connection to their meaning.
The only reason for a word is meaning.
You slew us one by one,
People by people,
Tribe by tribe,
Man,
Woman,
Child.

If you yearned for wisdom,
If you had need of understanding,
If you sought belief in the rising moon and the setting sun,
These are the things you should have taken.
We never owned the land.

Janet Dean is a Fellow of the Royal Society of Arts. She is a coach, mentor and facilitator in the public sector **www.deanknight.co.uk**, and lives with her family in York. Janet won the 2nd prize in the competition with this poem.

Arriving - Hull by Nicola Beeston

The view from this window,
Is leaden.
A weight.
Pressing down.
Cropped wet grass,
In long narrow gardens,
Bounded by thick high walls,
Surrounded by other high houses,
Long gardens, forbidding walls,
Shrunken trees that crane for light.
And rain.
Awful rain that oozes down
From the low grey skies
To the sodden ground.
And lies, in dirty puddles,
On black roofs and pavements.

The inner window,
Is a remembered landscape
Spread out in shimmering shades
Of umber and gold,
Stretching to far-off, visible horizons.
Space and light and heat
And that sense of freedom.

This sudden, terrible change.
She was going to hate it.
This terrible breathless fear.
That she would fail.
Simply because.
She could not.
Live.
Here.

Nicola Beeston was born and raised on a farm in Kenya which she loved very much. She now lives in England with her husband and her lurcher who together keep her sane.

Small Town Martians by Pierre Le Gué

Machines of Mars - I stood aside to let them pass
And as the last clanked by
Its driver raised a tentacle, so I waved back
Remembering the afternoon they came, apologetic
With their cylinder half -buried smoking in the cricket
pitch.
'We'll pay, of course'. 'Don't mention it,' we said.
'No lasting damage done, and after all,
It isn't every day we get a visitor from space.
Do you drink tea?'
They did, and so, it seems, did everyone on Mars.
'Our instruments detected it a century ago but you
Were in the middle of a war and so we had to go without
Till things calmed down a bit.'
Since they've been here, part of the village scene,
The parish fête just wouldn't be the same
Without the tripod rides and photographs.

Our Earth's unique they say - the only place
Within the Universe where some things now exist,
including tea.
'We'll take you to our leaders if you like,' somebody said.
'That's great, but could we have a brew before you do?'
So now, as well as a resort in France, a village in the Alps,
A South Pacific island, and a town near Washington DC
We're twinned with Mars, the only other world
Where they drink tea.

Pierre is a retired teacher who has been reading and
watching science fiction since 1947. He has had items
published in various poetry anthologies, specialist journals
and local newspapers. This is his second poem in the
collection.

Come to Rest by Farzana Marie

I have long been homeless.
Depending how many times
you've scraped your ankle
on the edge
you might know what I mean.

There is a patch of land we name,
usually, to answer the question
I've never understood,
a patch of land we claim saying
this one's mine.

But I found a mountain-land
with signs the people where I'm from
can't read,
where horse-carts mingle with Corollas,
where tea arrives alongside Coca Cola.

I found a desert-land that smells the same
after the rain as anywhere on earth,
where neither mud
nor missing limbs can stop kids
from playing ball.

I found a poem-land
whose words taste sweet
like yellow apricots in August,
where my soul comes to rest.
Tell me-where is home?

Farzana studies Persian Literature and serves as President of the non-profit **Civil Vision International**. She authored the book, '**Hearts for Sale! A Buyer's Guide to Winning in Afghanistan**' (2013). Farzana won third place in the competition and had three of her poems published. This is the first.

O England! By Robert J Miles

Won't you pile or pucker up your tweedy hills, make
toothy snares
of Green Man mouths, re-arm your Roman fortresses,
push up one
indignant boob and set a few more tacky tourist traps?

Won't you release your chalk hill horses and big-knobbed
giants, force
a filthy wave, pub-wipe that flash-capped beamer from his
perfect face
and scrumpy-kiss a wonky one on mine?

Won't you fold me back into your damp Sundays, keep me
safe
from he who dared to cross the pond and sway me,
commingle
with your chattering kind and gawp in awe at your
cathedrals?

Won't you swing your natty talk like hockey sticks, or fling
your history, entire museums of war, like enormous
drawers of cutlery
(working from the outside in, of course)?

Won't you hold his tongue so he might taste your basil,
spit his bazle
whence it came, rebut his 'erbs and re-preserve your gots
and haves,
resist his gotten this, his gotten that?

Won't you wuther-shrug him off your shawl of heather,
show him up
for his drawl and swagger? Cricket-whack him back, O
Ancient Mother!
Spare me from this beautiful New Englander!

One of our professional contributors, Robert grew up in
Devon and is based in Yorkshire. His poems have appeared
in pamphlets and journals. He's won firsts in several
international competitions; two were long listed for the
National Poetry Competition and one shortlisted for Live
Canon, 2012. Two also made the shortlist of the Wenlock
International, 2013.

Cuba by Pierre Le Gué

That month I thought we'd never see the spring.
With Castro and Khrushchev and Kennedy,
Cuba was on the map like nowhere else
In those few autumn days - just one weekend
That came and went so fast. The crisis grew.
We watched the news as hour by hour the ships,
The Russian fleet and JFK's blockade,
Seemed set to fight, then stopped - right on the brink
Of war. 'The other guy just blinked' they said,
But now we know that both sides saw the light
In time to make the world a safer place,
If only for a while. Between the crews
Bourbon and vodka passed instead of shells.
But - there'd be other times and other days
When ideologies and motherlands
Or fatherlands and leaders would recede,
And stark destruction move to centre stage
In people's minds. So far it's worked, but still
The danger lurks, and waits to be renewed
The moment memory fades, and wisdom learned
Falls foul of ignorance or arrogance and greed.

Pierre Le Gué is a retired teacher who has been reading and watching science fiction since 1947. He has had items published in various poetry anthologies, specialist journals and local newspapers. This is his third poem in the collection.

February Walks by Jo Reah

Orange lights
street lamps
Wet tarmac
Reflections
Memories
Dusk
Night
A torch.
Hedges
Trees
Cats
hiding
Dogs
sniffing,
Late walks
after tea
after work.
Dreams of
blossom trees
in April

Nature reserve
all blossom
No mud
along
the path.
This winter
the birds
have not
Fed
in my garden.

Jo Reah has been a poet all her life. Her love of nature and animals is reflected in her poetry, as is her experience of psychiatric illness and social isolation. Most of her life, she has lived in the north of England, though she has spent time in Sussex. She trained as a psychiatric nurse in Sedgewick, then moved to Manchester before settling in Sheffield where she now lives with her rescue dog, Milly.

Year after Year by Jo Reah

My grief lies deep beneath the autumn leaves,
decaying into the ground.
Year after year,
trodden into the mud
sodden and flat
skeletal patterns
surrounding my feet.
Year after year.
The same people
going their different ways,
welly-booted children
scurrying off to school,
kicking stones along the path.
Year after year.
The old man with his walking stick,
hovering over deliberate steps.
Harassed mothers pushing their infants
in prams loaded with shopping,
howling toddlers by their sides,
mittens dangling from coats.
Year after year.

College students in striped scarves,
arms hugged around books,
papers flapping from thick files.
The middle-aged lady with her new 'hair-do'
hanging on to her headscarf.
The town tramp trudging along dejectedly,
looking for 'fag-ends'...
bending over the gutter to spit,
a grey hulk leaning against the lamp-post
Year after year.
And in the cemetery, I knelt beside
my teacher's grave,
knowing that she would have flowers,
Year after year...

Jo Reah has been a poet all her life. Her love of nature and animals is reflected in her poetry, as is her experience of psychiatric illness and social isolation. Most of her life, she has lived in the north of England, though she has spent time in Sussex. She trained as a psychiatric nurse in Sedgewick, then moved to Manchester before settling in Sheffield where she now lives with her rescue dog, Milly.

Liberators by Pierre Le Gué

Such nice young men they were, or so I thought -
Grey uniforms and caps, and so polite.
They came with helmets on, in roaring trucks
And marched with drums and guns as we looked on
With cheers and waves. They said our little town
Belonged to Germany before the War -
They made it sound so very right and true.
To think that we were French a week ago,
And now it seems we're German once again.
I don't think I'm so sure now why they're here;
Those older men in charge don't smile at all.
A guard on every corner and our papers checked
Whenever we go to the shop for bread.
Not that there's much of anything around
Compared to how things used to be before.
We showered them with flowers, swallowed their line
Until it was too late, and here we are.
Now anyone who dares to say a word
About it all finds those polite young men
Don't seem so nice, Although they'd like to be, I'm sure.

Pierre Le Gué is a retired teacher who has been reading and watching science fiction since 1947. He has had items published in various poetry anthologies, specialist journals and local newspapers. This is his fourth poem in the collection.

Makuyu – Leaving by Nicola Beeston

To be permanently penned in this far corner,
Cut off from my own countryside:
The harsh, high cry of a hawk overhead,
And the chattering squabble of weaver birds
Flashing yellow in the swaying palm tree.
To long for the soft murmuring
Of the heat-relieving wind
Wafting across the open grass lands,
And the glimmer of a snow-glad peak,
Hovering mirage-like,
Between the vast sweep of sky and land.
This is my Greatest Fear.

To lose these special memories
Of the place that shapes and defines me
Of the land that creates my identity.

To forget the dawning symphony of birdsong,
The sweet evening serenade of crickets,
The lilac splendour of jacarandas
And the purple cascade of bougainvillea.
The sudden sinking of a blinding sun,
And the satin coolness of a star-spangled night.

To grow away from the memories that make me what I am,
Is like dying in pieces.
So I carry each fragile image
Enshrined in my heart,
Recalling each with tortured love
To arm me against the present horror of loss and change,
And the yet more permanent exile of forgetting.

Nicola Beeston was born and raised on a farm in Kenya which she loved very much. She now lives in England with her husband and her lurcher who together keep her sane. This is her second poem in the collection.

Russian Dolls by Janet Dean

I was an egg among many,
It was me she bore.
Long before she was born,
(Tangled in the chord of her Twin Sister),
Grandmother, (in whom my DNA lay),
Waited, patient as a Russian doll.

Her face, a waxing gibbous moon
Rising above the beer pumps polished by Great
Grandmother,
Blushed when young men rushed in,
Then married the one whose final letter came
Damp from the Somme.
She mourned at the bar.

Miners surging down the Dale trudged into the pub.
One consoling look took her mind away.
My Mother (and her Twin), were born of these
Disasters. One Death. One Disappointment.
Mother resented being the Daughter
Of the second-best, but we live

Inside each other.

Janet Dean is a Fellow of the Royal Society of Arts. She is a coach, mentor and facilitator in the public sector **www.deanknight.co.uk**, and lives with her family in York. This is her second poem in the collection.

Khoreji by Farzana Maric

Trying to buy two kilos of cucumbers in a sea
of open-air shops, I came face to face
with a Kabuli vender, gawking at my khoreji
height? eyebrows? stray hair-wisp? I took my time
to count the change, not make a mistake, escape his sight
as the blaze climbed my invisible neck, the pale neck of a
stranger.

In their carefully-messaged imaginations, or in stranger
realities, my countrymen had marched through minds that
could not see
me except as spectacle, a peculiar tourist site
imported to their neighborhood. My face
was still a fill-in-the-blank to them; in time,
I knew, we could know each other but how long must I be
a khoreji?

I still hear beautiful scarred children chanting khoreji,
khoreji,
a dirty word to me as I walked their dusty streets. Why
must I seem stranger
than others neighbor greeting, salaam? But no. Khello! Vat
time
Eez eet? Vat eez yor name? each clamoring for ruthless
courtesy,
innocently spelling out the sentence of a different face,
exiled to otherness for life (though not by any law that they
could cite).

I was so much like them; I always thought I could incite
them to believe it. I did not dress like a khoreji;
I went out fully cloaked, headscarf often masking half my
face.
I rarely ate khoreji foods sold on Chicken Street, as a
stranger
seeking familiarity in midst of foreignness might do. They
could see

that I drank tea and ate rice spiced with cumin, didn't
come on time,

and went to the hamaam or took a bucket-bath in
wintertime.
But it was the veil that obscured their sight,
the dark of distance clouding unsee-
ing eyes that cannot know truth about khorejis
from lies, until a word like 'friend' replaces 'stranger,'
until the foreign-specter departs the now-familiar face.

I thought one must be brave to face
the fact of otherness during one's time
as a khoreji. But by the end I was not such a stranger;
lounged over long dinners with friends pondering insights
on the ins and outs of the khoreji
phenomenon, and laughed at how at first neither could see

the other's face. After nine month's time
I returned to the land of khorejis, glad not to be a foreign
sight,
but found again a mass of strangers seeming not to see.

Farzana studies Persian Literature and serves as President of the non-profit **Civil Vision International**. She authored the book, '**Hearts for Sale! A Buyer's Guide to Winning in Afghanistan**' (2013).

Farzana won third place in the competition and had three of her poems published. This is the second in the collection.

Parepidemos by Farzana Marie

Something familiar
when you walk into town:
kids chase a rooster.
drying clothes flap in the sun,
old men play chess in the square.
They stare at first,
but later laugh with you
at the children's antics,
at your funny accent.

You settle,
never fully one of them
but woven like a new color of wool
into a hand-crafted kilim.

Nomads know what essentials are.
They wouldn't bring the kitchen sink
even if they had one.
Life is hard, whittled down
to its main ingredients.

It is so much easier to build a house
and fill it with packing peanuts.

After harvest-time, we build these sukkas:
a reminder to thank God for grains and fruits,
but also for our lives and freedom.
As rookie desert nomads,
we relied on Him for everything.
He travelled with us.

The young one peers at hanging grapes,
at palm branches weaving
the booth's roof,

wonders how God
could live in a tent.

In Kyrgyz lore, one must always ready
for the arrival of guests:
one guest especially.

If the Wanderer knocks on your door
you invite him in,
feed him your best pilaf and tea,
and he will leave a blessing for your home.
(If you don't, your home will be cursed.)

You might not know him right away,
but when he breaks the bread,
you will see his hands.
Then you will know.

Farzana studies Persian Literature and serves as President of the non-profit **Civil Vision International**. She authored the book, '**Hearts for Sale! A Buyer's Guide to Winning in Afghanistan**' (2013).

Farzana won third place in the competition and had three of her poems published. This is her third in the collection.

They looked back from the moon
by Pierre Le Gué

They looked back from the Moon to see their mother
world,
A blue glass marble held at arm's length in the sky
Against the unimaginable black of space
A black so rich and deep it was a colour in itself,
Made all the more so by the stars that sprinkled it;
Some showing tints of orange, pink or green
But mostly white, that rose and set above the close horizon
Of this far smaller world than ours that nobody called
home.
Their feelings varied – awe, elation, even fear perhaps
Passed through their minds, as they looked up at Earth.
Up there – down there – was all the history they knew
With science, maths, the whole curriculum in fact.
Geography too. Against the blue the sandy brown
Of land, and white cloud systems changing as they watched
That curved across the whole globe, linking continents.
But blue was the prevailing colour in the scene
And when they came back here that's what they said.
With all the colours of the stars, there's only one
That shines out like a bright blue jewel in space;
Our Earth, the only mother world we'll ever have.

Written in appreciation of an address given n 1987 by the
Rev. Col. James Irwin,
Apollo 15 Lunar Module Pilot, at St Cuthbert's Church,
Over Kellet, Lancashire.

Pierre Le Gué is a retired teacher who has been reading
and watching science fiction since 1947. He has had items
published in various poetry anthologies, specialist journals
and local newspapers. This is his fifth poem in the
collection.

Ghosts at your table
by Frances Andrews

Do you see me?
Waving from the corner of your home.
Grey and ghost like
The wraith at your table.
If you can't see me
How can you help?
Look at me, see me,
I am you, are you me?
I am your future and past.
War, famine and ignorance our common past.
Will you share the plenty of your homeland's future?
I ask so little from a rich man's feast.
Help me!
Peace I need.
Food I must have, clean water too.
Build me schools
Books not bombs.
Ask me in, take me in.
Let me sit at your table
And be your friend.
Together we will build a future
For all mother's children.

Frances Andrews is 63yrs old and lives in Worthing, West Sussex. She started writing poetry seriously about six years ago after she had to take early retirement due to ill health. She's owned by a small whitish cat!

What's in a Name?
by Brian Burchill

Look here upon this concrete mound
Of hopes encapsulated forty years before,
Their half-life some thousand years away
And mine already spent!
I remember all those aspirations
For a brave new world – the future bright,
Electricity cheap – the four-day week
And, 'leisure time' will be our prize!
Uranium, Plutonium – infinite resources
No need for Miners now to hack
Their lives away with silicosis.
Power for everyone, at little cost! ...
Besides – Fossil fuels won't last for ever,
Smog and chemicals pollute the air
Far better use clean nuclear power
And dump our waster somewhere...
Else...

For there's no problem we can't solve,
No place that can't be found
What we need now, we will have now,
What we don't – bury underground...
Somewhere –
As for going critical,
No need for fears of that.
It's all encased in a concrete shield
Two hundred and forty inches thick...
We'll damp it down a little more
Should the pile become too hot,
'Insert more rods into the core,
We'll keep it running sweet'...
If there is a problem; things go wrong,
And the media starts to lay blame,
We can sing the public relations song,
Give the place another name.
So – The Nuclear Age is here to stay
That's the moral of this story,
For there's no alternative they say
Man must have his power and...
The glory?

Brian Berisford Burchill (1932 – 2008)
Educated at Pinner Grammar School and Harrow School of Art. Began as a Technical Illustrator, Art Editor and then turned to teaching. Moved to Eastbourne as a freelance artist and exhibited his work around Sussex and taught at several evening centres. Later he combined this with people with learning difficulties. He combined both paintings and poetry inspired by Nature, Sussex coastline, Downs and countryside.

Movements by Brian Burchill

The sky, haze-hung, lowers over the sea
Of viridian slate; whilst the white horses,
Wind-driven, lunge landward searching the lee
Of distant shores to vent their force.
Seabirds wheeling, skimming the crests
Of waves, just out of reach;
Searching for food with no thought of rest,
Till sated and salted they line the beach.
Where, dun-coloured pebbles clack
Endless shifting – continuous labour
Push-pulled by tides, forward and back
Each scour, scarring itself and its neighbour.
I stand and watch, moved by the movement;
Observing, yet part of the scene
Which beginning, lasts but a moment
Never to regain what just now it had been.
On the horizon, ships that can scarcely be seen,
Chart their courses across the sea
Pale smoke-smudges, that mark where they've been
Fade and are no more to do with me.

To a brave unknown lady
by Brian Burchill

I did not know the lady
Nor even know her name
She died two weeks ago
- It will not be the same
But I knew her daughter;
And in her eyes writ plain,
All those feelings that had passed
Were shared, as was the pain.
Of the knowledge of what lay ahead;
Of being cheerful, knowing that she knew
'How it would be when she got better', but –
She knew that we did too.
This lady, nameless, faceless,
Unknown and no longer there
Somehow has touched upon my life,
I cannot help but care.
I did not know the lady
Nor even knew her name
She died two weeks ago –
It will not be the same.

THE END

We hope you enjoyed this collection and will continue to support it by telling your friends and **leaving a review**.

SPACE FOR **YOUR** THOUGHTS

SPACE FOR **YOUR** THOUGHTS

SPACE FOR **YOUR** THOUGHTS

SPACE FOR **YOUR** THOUGHTS

www.ingramcontent.com/pod-product-compliance
Lightning Source LLC
Chambersburg PA
CBHW071838020426
42331CB00007B/1779